The Art of Being Fly

Angel White

Copyright © 2019 Angel White
All rights reserved.
ISBN: 978-1-7342546-0-0

*To my beloved son Jason,
No matter what you choose to do with your
life strive to always be the hardest working
man in the room and when you are in that
room, also be the flyest.*

CONTENTS

Preface
pg. 9

1. NuNu Taught me
pg. 15

2. The Eb Effect
pg. 24

3. Ms. White
pg. 31

4. Ms. Trendsetter
pg. 37

5. SwaggerJackers
pg. 41

6. Essentials
pg. 46

7. The " IT" Factor
pg. 51

PREFACE

For as far back as I can remember, I've been drawn to fashion. The excitement I'd feel when I'd come across a piece I loved is almost indescribable and unmatched. The desire to have shoes no one else had or to be the best dressed on every set created a sensation for me like no other. A psychological analysis would say that I used fashion as a tool to fill a void in my life or that I was suppressing my childhood hurt and traumas or overcompensating. Well, I'm not a doctor, but all I know is that if I saw a piece I wanted, I had to have it. I couldn't sleep without it and once it was mine I would rock it like no other. That ability separated me permanently. It was my superpower, it made me "Her". Being "Her" meant that no one would be concerned about my race or what I didn't have, which included my father. It meant that all the things that made me cry at night no longer mattered. You see, because once you're "Her" no one cares about your flaws. Figuring that out made a very self-conscious, outcasted little girl become almost obsessed. I became a fashion freak.
Growing up we didn't really have it like

that. My mother would hate to hear this; I can see her rolling her eyes and cursing me out for even mentioning it but is what it is. Raising four kids on your own means that you have to be resourceful and do the best you can. So we wore what she could afford. She did her best and we always looked decent just wasn't fly, at least not to me. So, I was hype when my sisters could no longer fit something, I plotted on their shit and encouraged their demise so they could be mine. The eldest of the twins, my sister Alexis got a job at 16. I'm three years younger so her first job meant my first shot at the things I actually wanted. At 13 for me, as a tomboy, it was all about the sneakers! Just my luck she became a mini sneaker head after dating a guy who worked at a sneaker store. I'd watch in anticipation, picturing how I was going to stunt at school in her shit. All the torment was going to be over because I was going to be FLY. I couldn't control that I looked Chinese with big nappy hair and a face full of freckles or that everyone in my family was a different skin color but if I was fly it wouldn't matter! Sure, nowadays everyone loves afros, freckles, and anything different but when.
I was coming up, the last thing anyone wanted to do was be different. I remember

hating myself for it. Not a day went by where I wasn't called poor or Chinese in some sort of derogatory way. I remember just wishing I was one thing. One race. I didn't even care which race, I just wanted to look normal. I just knew that everything about me was wrong in the eyes of everyone else who saw me and it made me hate my life, hate my reflection. I was an alien. Not to mention that at that age what was on ya feet was way more important than what was in ya mind or even ya heart. No one cared how well you could read, write or make art. If you didn't have what everyone else had, it highlighted that you might not be enough. The irony in it is that we were all in public housing and our moms were struggling to get by but we were all still measuring who had more. So my sisters hand me downs gave me an advantage, or so I thought. It was finally my turn to get her red First Down. Oh how I coveted it, I wanted it, I needed it! I was gonna shut shit down in that thing! And when the time came, when she was finally mine, she made me into a joke. The secret had somehow gotten out and for some reason, this one boy (for tryin to play me he shall forever remain nameless) went in about me being so skinny. Then he exposed me for wearing my sisters Timbs that were two sizes too big LOL and her big ass coat. How'd he know? I laugh now but back then I was devastated, I will never forget that day. I walked home crying, angry at the world. How could it be so cruel with all of my many misfortunes that made me different, why'd I get this one? I didn't get it. But I would have my revenge. I had to get fly.

NUNU TAUGHT ME

I blame my cousin NuNu and Carrie Bradshaw. Them hoes literally changed my life. See before them, I was just a tomboy only interested in climbing trees and competing against boys. I was that girl who detested the idea that a male was superior. This was my focus. Proving that anything they could do I could do. I was going to change the world. I reunited with my cousin NuNu around the age of 12. NuNu is my Aunt Crystal's middle child just like me. My mom had three girls and a boy. Her older sister, my Aunt Crystal, had three girls and a boy. So whenever my family decided to cross state lines to get together we would be paired up with our assigned cousin and mines was NuNu!

We didn't care, I'm pretty sure we came up with the concept because I couldn't wait to be with her, and for some strange reason, she liked being around me too. Everything about NuNu was perfect. Her room, how she talked, her hair, all of it but especially her clothes. She had this, *"FUCK YOU I'M FLY AND IMA BE SEXY IN YA FACE BUT WEIRD AND DIFFERENT IN A WAY NO ONE ELSE ON EARTH COULD, BUT WHEN I DO ITS DOPE AS FUCK"* type of style. And I wanted it. It was magnetic. Mysterious. You'd never know what the fuck NuNu was going to come out the house wearing. But it was always fly, always crisp, never dusty, and never forced. Her style is like air. I call it effortless fly. She had so much of it. I wanted to be just like her. I remember rolling my eyes at my mom wondering, why the fuck we had to be poor? I think right then and there is when I decided I would grow up to be rich. I had to be. Back to NuNu, she'd fuck you up because she'd pop out, dripped in her Stacey Dash from Clueless shit (before we canceled her) swinging her long, perfectly wrapped hair while talking like a valley girl but telling her friends on the phone about how someone looked like a straight bamma and got dragged for trying her. That was NuNu, so complex. I decided that was the only way to be. I remember being 16 and I couldn't wait for Thanksgiving so I could flex for her in my new olive green Rocawear Eskimo coat that I had saved up for, thinking I was shittin on em in my lil Enyce sweat-suit. She indulged me and praised me for my newfound fly. I wasn't satisfied though, I felt small. Her closet full of Chanel, Prada and Fendi seemed to mock me. I felt childish. She was goals before there were IG goals. I'd get there soon though. Around that same time was when I was introduced to Carrie Bradshaw. Having been a complete alien most of my life I remember every time that I saw myself in someone else. You never forget the ones that inspired you to just be you when the world had been telling you that you were wrong. I'd see it a few more times once I got older in Tracey Ellis Ross, Issa Rae, Lena Dunham, Erykah Badu and Cardi B; all icons who in some way contributed to my confidence and freedom to just be me. Carrie was a writer. I was a writer. That alone was huge. I had been winning awards for essays & poetry since the 2nd grade. I was the girl who people paid to write their papers in school but there wasn't anything cute about that. I never considered it special, if anything it was the opposite. I was almost embarrassed about it. I wanted to be the pretty, rich and popular girl. Instead, I was this Asian looking kid with a fro, freckles, bo-bo's and a deep voice. Boys liked boobs and butt, not brains and I had neither. But then comes Carrie with this whole life revolving around the same gift that I had and not just in a minute way. She was a big deal; she wrote for a newspaper, had her own column, and eventually secured a book deal! My bitch was on the side of a bus OK! She took it to a level my mind had not even conceived up until that moment. She made being a writer fly. Carrie had wild crazy hair. I had wild crazy hair. The similarities just stacked up and although I was a late bloomer when it came to a sex life, fashion-wise, I got my cherry popped at 14. Thanks to Carrie I bought a pair of Manolo Blahniks from a thrift store for $100. You couldn't tell me shit. I think I wore them until they were unwearable. You know when the heel has worn down to the metal and when you walk you hear that scraping noise? Yeah, I wore em like that. But even that couldn't stop me. I was on to the next thing I had no business wanting. Carrie's relationship with fashion opened a whole new world to me. I was Carrie, except I was 14, Black, broke & a virgin. But nevertheless, I was her, stacking up whatever dollar I earned to purchase Manolo, Jimmy Choo & anything that was difficult to pronounce. It was bad. I had a serious problem. But in the words of Carrie Bradshaw, "I like my money right where I can see it, hanging in my closet." When I began traveling as a model for hair and fashion shows it only made things worse. I got exposed to so much unique fashion at such a young age and I had fallen in love. There were designers like Nate from my hometown who used me as his muse for years and included me into his creative process. Learning what he could do with textures and colors was priceless and it took my talents and love to a whole new level. Soon after high school, I became a mother and although I worked full time I was also in school full time. Trying to pull that off turned out to be easier said than done. I excelled in every class when I did the work, but it was balancing it all that I repeatedly failed at. But the gift and the curse during that whole college experience was the student loans. Yes, I was paying tuition and books but what else was my loan financing? My closet! I told ya'll I had a problem, right? Ok, so stop judging me. You want to learn about the art of this here thang so I'm explaining what forced me to develop such an art. I would get my checks and after paying what I needed to pay, I would splurge. I don't mean your typical shopping spree, oh no I developed such a taste for high fashion that that was all my eyes could see. Gone were my days of Aldo, Arden B. and Nine West. If it wasn't difficult to pronounce then I didn't want it. Simultaneously, my modeling career had built such a name for me that I was now being booked to host events. Now, this was before the days of Instagram models being paid to solely sit pretty at clubs. In fact, this was kind of unheard of at the time. The role of an event MC or host went to the men in my hometown but my name got so big that now every promoter had to have Angel White on their ticket. Although it was flattering and helped grow my name tremendously, it was a lot of pressure. Remember, I was just a tomboy who after puberty happened to turn out aite looking. So although I was being praised for my unique looks and being paid well for these gigs, inside I was still just that broken, insecure little girl. The realization that I had a reputation to keep up with only added to my anxiety. See, although that word is quite popular now it wasn't then so I had no clue what was going on with me. All I knew was that life was kicking my ass and now I had a baby depending on me to kick it back. I understood that although I was being booked for my hosting abilities and name I was mostly being booked for my looks. My fly. So although I had teams that would keep my hair and makeup on point to help build their brands, the big chunk of my look would be what I wore. I had created such an expectation for myself that I would be up at night, breaking out in hives and making myself physically sick trying to beat out my only competition, myself. Struggling financially made it even harder. I had no manager or investor and there was no one paying me extra for the cost of my pieces so I had to figure it out. Luckily, because of my years on the runway and doing modeling jobs for people all over the town, I ended up having great relationships with boutique owners and stylists who would hunt me down to style me for my appearances. Relationships are key. Outside of that, I would rob from Peter to pay Paul like a motherfucker. That would result in years of credit card debt and more bad decision making surrounding money but damn it, it was worth it because I was fly.

Everyone would grow to know Angel White for her hustle, her creativity, her brains, her don't take any shit from no one attitude, and most of all, for her fly. That was the goal. I literally built myself into who I wanted to be. I was now HER.

*"People will stare.
Make it worth their while."*

—*Harry Winston*

THE EB EFFECT

> *" It's kind of fresh you listen to more than hip-hop and I can catch you in the mix from beauty to thrift shop plus you shit pop when it's time to,"*

I swore Common was talking about me and my crew. It went over many heads but for us, it was validation. It was our secret being exposed but respected. I had been put on to thrift stores at a young age, again remember we were poor so it was nothing for us to be up in Goodwill. And yeah as a kid I hated that shit trying to cover my face as my mom would drag us to look for school clothes. I didn't want a soul to catch me in there. But at some point in life that switched and I realized that the best presents were found there. Christmas. Especially once I became friends with Eb.

Ebonee is one of my bestest friends on this planet and has been since I was like 16. She came into my life when I first hit the scene as the shiny new model. Back then hair shows and fashion shows were life. As for the models, we were ghetto superstars. All the men loved us and all the women wished they could be us. When it was my time when to join I instantly, unexpectedly became the "It Girl." My big curly hair and brown freckles that I grew up hating were now the dopest shit ever. I was so confused. I remember it being like someone pressed a button and gave me confidence. You see internally I was having this conflict. Up until this moment I hated myself. Growing up none of the boys liked me; shoot I didn't even like me. I use to pray to look like everyone else, anyone else but me. But here, in this new world, I was it. I would overhear the older women and men making comments and I would catch them looking at me in ways that took me a while to read. But it was an encouraging look, or a whisper that grew to be loud that I was not ugly and weird but that I was special, that I was going to be the one to make it out. Although I noticed what they were saying, I didn't instantly get it or develop confidence. I got it through watching other girls like

Adryanna, Kandice, Pam, Eb and Sylvia. They were only a few years older than me but they were grown women. The way they dressed and carried themselves was magnetic like NuNu. They had such beauty and class without trying. Savoir-faire is what my mother calls it. I wanted to be just like them. I remember seeing them and wanting to have that confidence. The little tomboy who spent her life fighting boys and climbing trees realized she had it all wrong. Over time we'd all become friends. We were a huge group of models who lived like hood socialites. But one of the ones who stuck by my side as I blossomed into myself, was Ebonee. Most know her as @eboneepearl on Instagram for her amazing chain dresses & jewelry. She was my walking diary. See, Eb had next level looks and personality. That's what made her so dope. For one she was a teenager with this hourglass shape like no other. But she wasn't just her looks, her personality shined on the outside. She had this ability to make everyone feel special even if for a brief moment. She exuded beauty, confidence & kindness. She was never stank actin, you know. I would watch as we'd enter a room and I'd know firsthand about this girl or that girl who didn't like her, usually over a guy (always over a guy).

She would enter into a room and these girls would shrink, not just figuratively but literally. It was her confidence. She didn't see them hoes and all they wanted to do was be seen but couldn't be because everyone was too busy looking at Eb. Not just because of her physical features but also because of what she had on. I describe her style as the Sex Kitten. No matter what she put on it was always sexy even sweat pants. It was always unique and fly even way back then. I call her matchy matchy and I'm the weirdo who rarely matches but she is and has always been the ying to my yang. She is the thrift store queen. The back story is that at the young age of 14, Eb became a mother to an amazing set of twins and what most young moms know or eventually learn is to become very resourceful. This is how Eb fell into the thrift stores. When she relocated to Connecticut, she evolved into the thrift store master. See back in Rochester we had like one boutique, and three malls. If you're a fashionista, you understand that doesn't give you a lot of options. Much like myself, Eb had this horrible phobia of having on the same outfit as someone else, which in Rochester, New York happens all the time. But if you were the less fortunate person to end up in the same fit as Eb you'd be pissed because hers would always look different, always look better. A natural creative to her core, she couldn't just buy something and wear it as it was advertised, oh no. Nine times out of ten, she's going to cut the sleeves off, make it into a half-shirt, cut the pants up, something was getting done to it! She always buys things for their potential. She'd say she could see its possibilities as opposed to what it was. Eventually the idea of paying full price for something she was going to essentially break down and cut up started to make no sense. The realization that thrift stores were the resting place of tons of one of a kind, vintage, timeless treasures took shopping to a whole another level. It became like a sport and me being her bestie I got to benefit from all that knowledge. She doesn't just randomly shop, oh no, there's a whole strategy to it. She'd go on Sundays, not only was it her day to unwind and breathe but she soon learned that on Sundays everything is half off! She made it a rule of thumb to be there when the doors opened on Sunday mornings to get the full effect. It's like a high, like robbing a bank and getting away with it every single Sunday going home richer but the cops ain't coming lol. It's such an exhilarating feeling knowing this shit is gonna be cheap as hell (price-wise) but dope as fuck. Over the years we'd get a kick out of going out and standing next to someone in designer from head to toe outfit that costs thousands and here we are thrifted from head to toe but honey looking like a bag okkkuurrrr! I mean a bigger bag than they could ever buy because swag is everything and many times money cannot compensate for swag. Meanwhile our whole fit was like $20. Over the years, I would implement her skills when dressing and like to call this technique, *The Eb Effect*. There are three rules to *The Eb Effect:*

1. Study the thrift & retail stores in your area and learn when they have discounts and new items out. Do your research.

2. Always, always clean your items before wearing them thrift stores tend to carry a scent and no one wants to walk around smelling like mothballs.

3. Level Up. If you see something dope think of what you can do to it to make it doper. Think outside of the box.

"I think there is beauty in everything. What 'normal' people perceive as ugly, I can usually see something of beauty in it."

—*Alexander McQueen*

MS. WHITE

don't know where I initially got it from, whether it was NuNu or Carrie or the fact that I had a much older boyfriend who had a set standard for how I should look (we'll talk about that in my next book). But for as far back as I could remember I understood the concept of looking classy and sophisticated as opposed to gawdy and tacky. We all know those celebs who we all know are rich but every time we see them they look a hot mess. It's not because they don't care or aren't trying, that's usually the flaw - they're trying too hard and it shows. I won't name them because I don't down talk, but you know who I'm talking about because as soon as you read my words their image popped in your head LOL. Yeah, that person. They haven't learned the art they simply got to the bag and now buy whatever they think screams money, not realizing that money doesn't usually scream money, it just it.

Through fashion I would embody that. I would just be. My fits allowed me to use my creativity but at the same time it allowed me to become this whole other persona, a wealthy one, sexy, confidant & unique, a classic; Ms. White. She would always stand out, always looked like money but never gawdy. She didn't enter a room she glided and took ownership. Think of J Lo, Charlize Theron, Ciara, Rihanna, Cardi B, Beyonce, Solange, Monica, and Janelle Monae. The list goes on to my fashion faves but the theme for me is always simple but brave - fearless fashionistas. These are my picks for who embodies classic but unique fashion. Who are yours? For the aspiring fashionista reading this and still developing your style, look at those in the game, figure out who speaks to you and why. I love a classic look. The key is to not get caught up on price tags. That way of thinking is a joke. I may have gone broke a few times in the name of fashion but because of that, I learned tricks and rules to make sure it never happened again. It also had to be worth it. If you're going to run up a check in the name of fly shit make sure it's worth it. You should only be copping pieces. These objects are investments. Timeless. They last forever. These are the things you can't live without. The object that floats in your mind long after you've walked out of the store. Now if you're rich then you're probably uninterested in this part because you can buy whatever whenever but if you're like moi who has Rick Owens taste but sometimes a Chuck Taylor budget then this is for you. A true fashion freak knows about highs and lows. Their whole closet is full of highs and lows. For me it's all about the shoe. I can't go low in that department but it may be different for you. Maybe it's all about the bag for you. It is not unlike me to have on a pair of boots that retail $2,500 in a $10 Fashion Nova dress. That's just my flex. And not just Fashion Nova but there are tons of boutiques now that offer dope, cute, perfectly fitting pieces for the low low. H&M and Target are two of my other secret spots. But the key to finding fashion in these places is simplicity. Stay away from remakes or copies of high fashion because those tend to come out looking quite cheesy. If you stick to the basic, simple looks you can't go wrong. Think Kim K. Much of that isn't necessarily what you're wearing but how you're wearing it. Act like you've had some shit before - couth. That alone is some rich bitch shit, dripping without stating that you're dripping. Maybe I'm just old fashioned.

I love fashion and I love sophistication but I'm from the bottom of the bottom so even as I acquired designers I never felt comfortable being braggadocious or trying to make others feel small because of their lack. It's frustrating to admit but its true. People associate being fly with being mean or conceited and it's so the opposite. A key to this here thing is to be a humble fashionista. Balance = cocky humbleness. That is a skill of this art that many will ignore but oh how you will learn that fly inside is just as essential as being fly outside. Your fashion says all that needs to be said. That's when you know you've got it. You don't have to say anything let your look and your ambiance speak for you. Those moments will create distinct moments that will never be forgotten.

Some of my fave fashion moments:

1. Carrie's wedding
2. Carrie in a tutu on the bus for the ad for her column styled by Patricia Fields
3. Cardi B's red Thom Browne feather Met Gala gown
4. J Lo at the Grammys in her Versace gown
5. Rihanna in her Chinese couture yellow robe by Guo Pei at the Met Gala
6. Rihanna in full Bishop's mitre and cloak from the house of Maison Mariela remake at the Met Gala
7. Jeanette Chaves Styled by June Ambrose in Paco Rabanne dress in Jay-Z video
8. Lil Kim in mermaid style purple sequin catsuit & pasty designed by Misa Hylton
9. Hov & Bey in colorful fitted suits in front of the Meagan Markel painting
10. Clueless the entire movie

"Elegance is not standing out, but being remembered."

—Giorgio Armani

MS. TRENDSETTER

In 2006 I believe it was, I competed in a cross city competition called Mr & Ms. Trendsetter. There were different categories of competition and run way walking that included teens and young adults in Buffalo & Rochester. The completion highlighted personal style and confidence. That year I won 3rd place and the following year the over all crown was mine. Thus began my official reputation for fashion in Upstate, New York. As time would pass I would continue to win such titles and make statements with my appearances so much so, that people started to pay me to come shopping with them. I would literally go to the mall with them or look online depending on the event and help get them right. I wasn't an official stylist or anything although I did think about it for a quick second. But I didn't like the idea of doing it as work I just loved doing it and the money just made it better. Often when helping others I get asked about trends- people usually want to know the same thing. How do I stay on trend without looking trendy?

The question stumped me at first. I really couldn't put it into words because it seemed like common sense. But I soon realized it was not. Fashion freaks follow fashion so faithfully that they're constantly reading and seeing images of what's in and what's out, but who determines that? Once it's in, how do you know when it's out? The concept to me always seemed so opposite of why I loved fashion to begin with, so much so that I eventually rebelled completely against the notion altogether. I decided to write my own rules and encourage every fashion freak to do the same. What is the art of being fly? Being You. You over them. It's not cliché, its fact. Some of the most fly cultural icons and even people from your everyday life are the people who have the confidence to just be themselves. Those are the ones we remember, not the ones that looked like everyone else. Fashion is timeless, everything is always in style. Nothing is old and that's the beauty of it. Yes, you might pay some money but it's a part of your collection FOREVER. I am a firm believer in wearing and remixing items in your collection. For the baby fashion freaks who are still figuring themselves out, don't fret, the truth is that there is no time limit. You can always reinvent yourself and switch your style up at any given moment. It's your God-given right! So test the trends, try them on, see what you hate on you but love on others. Be adventurous but with great caution because in the words of the great Karl Lagerfeld, "Trendy is the last stage before tack." So yes, study fashion. Know the trends. Test the trends but in the end, your style and what you choose to wear is like a blank canvas each day. Create a fresh Instagram page with not a single post. Each outfit is a new opportunity to say who you are. Challenge yourself to live freely in that. Sometimes that will include what's in style and what the public is saying is trendy and that's okay as long as when you look in the mirror you smile and feel like the baddest bitch. That is all that matters. The art of being fly translates into the art of being yourself.

"Don't be into trends. Don't make fashion own you, but you decide what you are, what you want to express by the way you dress and the way to live."

— ***Gianni Versace***

SWAGGERJACKAS

There is a thin line between being inspired and swagger jacking. On this journey of self-discovery, developing your style and falling in love with the styles of others, you will feel moved. At the moment you will decide to salute a real one and go about your business or you will decide you want that essence for yourself. You will take back the concept and regroup it as you recall and then make the obvious choice to either simply sketch it out, screenshot it and smile or you will decide when and where you will wear this new fit. As no idea is original, the whole notion of copycatting can be quite controversial all together but here's my take. Who fuckin cares. No one is you and that baby is your power! No one can do what Angel White does, PERIODT! That has been my philosophy with fashion out the gate. In the beginning years, however, if you copied me, it was beef. No bullshittin. To me that was a clear sign that I was being challenged and just like a lioness in the jungle, it was permanently on. Biting my shit was like fighting words. As I grew up God decided to make a once grudge-holding petty queen into an empathetic, understanding lady. Magnanimous in every way I and began contemplating the motives and intentions of others in a way that truly changed me. I started to not take it personally and understand that imitation is the highest form of flattery. In that, I began to look at my truth of inspiration - Selena, Rihanna, Lil Kim, Kelis, Left Eye, Aaliyah, and J Lo. These are all icons I mimicked at some point in my life much like every girl my age (if she says she didn't, she's fronting). I copied every single bloodclot ting that Queen Bey did. She can do no wrong so if Bey did it, I had to try it. I soon realized that some of my inspirations weren't even about fashion at all. No one on tv looked like me, not even a little bit. The closest examples were Asian women whose bodies and hair textures were completely opposite of mine and while I knew I was black, I didn't know any other black girl nor did I see any in magazines or tv that looked like me. I was an alien so my strategy was to change what I could. I would get relaxers to straighten my hair or constantly wear weaves. It wasn't until I kept seeing Carrie Bradshaw, Kelis and Tracy Ellis Ross thrive in their careers with big curly-headed dopeness that I began to see beauty in my natural hair just as the latest beauty trend of fake freckles made me see beauty in the mirror as opposed to a discoloration that I needed to cover up. I fell in love with lilac hair from Kelly Osbourne initially but was hesitant because of my hair's texture. I didn't think black girls could do their hair like that until Heather Sanders. She bodied it years before I did. She gave me the confidence to go for it and I've been stuck with it ever since. Going from a big curly fro to a short cut was inspired by Kelis. I even took it a step further and began to feel inspired to show my personality more on social media because of Cardi B. Prior to her I was on this quest to hide my "ratchet side" thinking that I wouldn't be accepted in the business world if they knew who I really was. It was through her rise that helped me to see what I've always known - that God made each of us uniquely and wonderfully, therefore, we should all embrace authenticity on every level. What's for you will gravitate to you, not from you. The list goes on and on of looks I stole or tried to remix after seeing my favorite fashion freak so I had to humble myself and think who am I to judge. We all are inspired by someone at some point in life. It's the fashion ones that are so obvious to the eye but nevertheless, fashion has no rules. Some of you reading this are swagger jackers and when you finish this chapter, it might be the first time you realize it. And that's ok. Those that can't do a copyright? I don't know about all that but here is my alternative theory. Get inspired but always think of a way to level up a look by making it your own. Figure out your esthetic and how you can always own a look no matter who did it first because no one likes a fucking copy cat.

"In order to be irreplaceable one must always be different."

—*Coco Chanel*

ESSENTIALS

Kandice aka @kanz on Instagram is another fashion freak friend of mine that I have always admired and someone you should know. She bodied the concept of classic looks and remixing a fit. Kandice would wear and re-wear shit, add shit, cut shit and make it look brand new. She had this eye for dope shit like none other. She'd dress the other girls in our crew like we were on set of a photoshoot. Every day though! This was our real life even if we were only walking up the street to the corner store it was a moment and Kandice was going to make sure no man was left behind LOL. No one would get caught slipping. This was before the days of Instagram people, so you have to understand the dedication and lack of appreciation. But we didn't care. We literally would set up shop with bins and suitcases full of all our goods and just camp out at one of the houses for days, even weeks at a time. This was way before we became mothers and fully developed into ladies. This was that weird age for women when we are fresh out of high school so all the grown men are hounding and keeping track of our hips spreading but we are still actually goofy little girls on the inside. Our entire life revolved around the next fashion show or club appearance because both were our playgrounds. The rest of the world was merely our audience. Our entrance made the party a party and we knew it. The hood started calling us Model Mafia and at one time we were like a family. Everything we did was a WE factor or with US in mind. I think that's why I clung to it. They were my sisters in my eyes and there wasn't anything I wouldn't do for them. That included sharing my shit. We all did. Yeah, yeah, now that shit is dirty and we grew out of it on the same timeline of us growing apart but back then we were kids and yes we shared clothes. That made our selection so much more eclectic. We had a plethora of tops, bottoms, belts and accessories and everyone was down for the cause of the look. We didn't give a damn what you borrowed from one another, it was our job to see it through. Kandice and I would sometimes clash in debates on my style because I am so stubborn and a die-hard about my individual esthetic. I would smart motherly tell her, "No boo, you dress them, not me. I do this!" But the truth is, I always admired her opinion and passion. My ego just wouldn't let me tell her. Honestly, I can't recall her ever having a fashion fail, ever. I was fly but she was too. We were both bulls. I'd describe her overall esthetic at the time as being a master at how to stock a closet. Amanda Williams was the queen of that too. The world knows her as the inspirational prayer warrior whose whole life is goals, but I know her as Amanda Gutierrez. One thing she always did back then and still does to this very day is know how to put together a look on a budget. Amanda was not with that going broke for fashion. Instead she had the eye like Kandice. They knew how to maximize off of what they had and knew just what to add to look that little bit of extra. They knew how to stock a closet like no other. Closet essentials can make or break a wardrobe, especially in the case of styling for a shoot or traveling where you never know what can happen. Always being prepared is key to avoid a fashion crisis. I learned that from both of them.

Closet essentials that easily create classic looks:

1. black blazer
2. oversized men's white button-up
3. lumberjack shirt
4. solid black heel
5. black leggings
6. trench coat
7. denim jacket
8. Yankee fitted
9. black dress
10. perfect fit jean

With these items in your suitcase or closet you can be prepared for anything. Maybe as you go along you'll create your own list that might differ from mine but the point is to always be prepared. If you stay ready you ain't gotta get ready.

"Being well dressed hasn't much to do with having good clothes. It's a question of good balance and good common sense."

—*Oscar de la Renta*

THE "IT" FACTOR

Sometimes, the only thing missing in a look is something missing. Confusing right? Not really. Once you train your eye to look for "it" you will know "it' every time you see it. Sometimes moving a fit from basic cute to fly is as simple as the right shoe or an accessory. Accessories are the most understated overstatement. It is the second chance to let your personality shine. During my Model Mafia days, once I made us into a legitimate business, I decided we needed that it factor for our appearances. So I jacked Carrie's "pin a flower on your shirt" method. If you somehow missed it, I first need you to binge-watch every season of Sex and the City. I need you to pay special attention to season 3 when she wore giant Chanel flowers pinned to her shirts. So what did we do? We went to Walmart and bought up the biggest flowers we could find and glue gunned our way into Rochester fashion history. As an option to switch it up we'd wear huge bowties. I personally thought it was genius. And ever since then I've always been an accessory girl. The Carrie in me constantly needs to have on a crown or vintage belt, something extra to give me that "it". Now everyone's version of it varies so don't be compelled to think that you too now have to go all Carrie on em. That's the whole trick, figuring out your "it" and understanding that what makes me Angel is going to be different for you. That's the whole point. Doing you. Being fearless to test things out and take risks. There is no better way for an individual to express themselves artistically than with fashion because it's limitless, freeing.

So what is the Art of Being Fly?

1. Embrace your flaws
2. Shop consignment
3. Level up - make dope things doper
4. Classic > Gawdy
5. Invest in classic, pricier pieces
6. Purchase simple pieces at online boutiques, Target and H&M
7. Balance = Cocky Humbleness
8. Wisely stock your closet with essentials
9. Use accessories to create your "IT Factor"
10. Be yourself and use fashion to express who you are

Throughout my career, I was constantly mocked and made fun of for my fashion choices then followed years later by the praise of those same choices. I've been the subject of fake pages created solely to make fun of things I've worn only to have those same choices glorified months later in Vogue, (true story). Not to mention, (my bf's are my witnesses) on more than one occasion, I've sketched out full clothing collections that I never produced only to see them years later being debuted at NYFW. The moral of the story is, fuck these people.

Do You. It all boils down to you. I can write book after book telling you what I think is fly and who I think is fly but when it's all said and done it's up to you. It's what your eyes see and how fashion speaks to you. Are you moved by fabric and colors, texture and feel? Is fashion your career or just your soft spot? There is no right or wrong answer and there is no blueprint for being fly. It's impossible to create such a blueprint because the ink evaporates and takes form in different directions depending on the architect. There is no blueprint, it's an art. Each brush stroke is unique and essential. You have to own your clothing and pieces like you own your skin, your facial features and body curves. You have to never bow down to another opinion on fashion so much so, that you'd dare put down a piece that your heart told you to pick up. The art of being fly is a beautiful song and dance with a poetry intro that sounds like an iconic rap verse you've never heard but somehow know the beat.

"Fashion you can buy, but style you possess. The key to style is learning who you are, which takes years. There's no how-to road map to style. It's about self-expression and, above all, attitude."

—Iris Apfel

ABOUT THE AUTHOR

Angel White, the poet also known as blog writer, The Freckled Muse resides in both Rochester, New York and Atlanta, Georgia. Her poetry can be heard on her 2019 project, The Muse Tape. Her artwork, writing, interviews, books and merch collection are available on MsAngelWhite.com. The Art of Being Fly, is a humorous yet factual account of her journey creating a name for herself through fashion. Throughout Angel's career, as a teen model turned media personality she would go on to win many awards & best-dressed mentions including being crowned Ms. Trendsetter of Buffalo & Rochester, New York. While conducting interviews she would often find herself being questioned by the celebs on her look & style which left on impression everywhere she went. The Art of Being Fly explains how she did just that and acts as a How-to Guide for fashion lovers everywhere especially those on a budget.

For performing, public appearances or press:
info@msangelwhite.com
IG: msangelwhite
www.MsAngelWhite.com

Made in the USA
Monee, IL
20 January 2020